A Bible Study

Paul's Letter to the Romans

Written by Participants in the
Holy Spirit Institute
Detroit, Michigan
2001 - 2004

ISBN 0-939241-38-2

Developed for use by:

The Detroit Catholic Charismatic Renewal Center
Arlene Apone, Director
Archdiocese of Detroit
1390 Quarton Road
Bloomfield Hills, MI 48304

Phone: (248) 593-4888
Fax: (248) 593-4889
E-mail: dccrcenter@aol.com

Acknowledgments:

As a work project, ten students of the four year program called the "Holy Spirit Institute," met every first Saturday of the month for one year, and combined their prayerful insights into a study on the Book of Romans.

They continued to meet monthly for a second year, and took the Bible Study themselves to experience the fruits of their labors.

They all agreed the Lord continues to teach His people through the Scriptures, and very specially through the Book of Romans.

I wish to acknowledge the following persons as the co-authors of this Bible Study on Paul's Letter to the Romans:

Darlene Czop
Agnes Fedewa
Ila Mae Lancendorfer, Editor
Cynthia Mallory
Kathryn Marcell
Linda Olsowy
Cecylia Powers
Victoria Samuelson
Deborah Tourville
Neives Vargas

I am grateful to them for their faithfulness and dedication to the composition and refining of this Bible Study, all enveloped in their ongoing, deep prayer.

Arlene Apone
Faculty Member of the Holy Spirit Institute
Director of, as well as Contributor to, this Project

Preface

HOW TO READ THE BIBLE

Slowly and carefully, read a passage in the Bible.

Then, ask the following questions about the passage and write out the answers:

1. What did I hear? (Summarize the essence of the passage just read.)

2. How does it affect me? (Apply what was read to one's own personal life.)

3. What is my prayer? (Address the Lord directly with words that come from the heart and are motivated by thoughts from the Scripture passage.)

4. Ask the Lord, "Is there anything else about which You want to speak to me today?"

A Bible Study

Paul's Letter to the Romans

Read **Chapter 1:1-32,** then answer the following questions:

1. How does my faith bring me new life?

2. Concerning others:

    a.   In what ways do I share the gospel message with others?

b. In what ways do I support/encourage others in their faith and in what ways am I supported/encouraged?

3. How does the power of the "Word" strengthen me personally in my relationship with God and others?

Read **Chapter 2:1-29,** then answer the following questions:

1. In regard to myself:

    a.   What have I learned about myself?

    b.   How has this self knowledge affected me?

2. Has God's kindness and mercy changed my heart and
   attitude toward others? Explain.

3. How interested would others be in learning more about
   God after observing me?

Read **Chapter 3:1-31,** then answer the following questions:

1. Each of us has our own faith journey. Write out your personal faith journey using a timeline. How has God revealed His faithful love?

2. Regarding salvation:

   a.   Why does humanity need God's salvation?

b. What is the role of Jesus in this salvation?

3. In light of Christ's blood shed for me on Calvary, how prepared am I for my death?

Read **Chapter 4:1-25,** then answer the following questions:

1. God justified Abraham because Abraham trusted in God's promises. How do I trust in the promises of God?

2. What or who helps me to maintain or increase my level of faith?

3. Our righteousness (blamelessness due to faith that is working effectively) does not depend on our self-effort but on God's gift in Jesus Christ. In what ways do I rely on my own efforts?

Read **Chapter 5:1-21,** then answer the following questions:

(See "The Holy Spirit and Salvation" in Appendix I on p. 35.)

1. (vs. 5): *"And this hope is not deceptive, because the love of God has been poured into our hearts by the Holy Spirit which has been given us."* The Holy Spirit is God's pledge to us of salvation.

   a. Who is the Holy Spirit?

   b. What work has been given to the Holy Spirit?

2. St. Paul tells us in vs. 8 that the gift of the cross brought acquittal of all transgressions, and we become justified.

    a.   Whom do I consider a justified person?

    b.   How does it make me feel to know that God's love and grace acquitted me by the cross of Jesus Christ?

3. Once having sinned, how can I return to the peace I had before I sinned; what have I learned through the struggle?

Read **Chapter 6:1-23,** then answer the following questions:

1. What does it mean to me to be a new creation in Christ?

2. In what ways do I allow the Holy Spirit to teach, guide, and transform me in my journey of sanctification?

3. How do I share in the paschal mystery of Jesus' death and resurrection?

Read **Chapter 7:1-25,** then answer the following questions:

1. What does it mean to live according to the law?

2. How does serving God in the *"way of the Spirit"* differ from serving God *"by the letter of the law?"* Why was the law important?

3. How do I relate to Paul's remarkable confession of the inward struggle he experienced? Share if possible.

Read **Chapter 8:1-39,** then answer the following questions:

1. What does it mean to live according to the Spirit?

2. How do we become heirs of God?

3. If nothing can separate us from the love of God then why do we still have fears, and what are they? Personally, what are my greatest fears?

Read **Chapter 9:1-33,** then answer the following questions:

1. Who are the true descendants of God and what does God promise them?

2. What is said about God's mercy?

3. In light of God's love and mercy:

   a.   What is the depth of my love and concern for those who have not yet accepted God's saving justice?

b. How is God's love for all people reflected in my actions?

4. We are to trust God. How docile am I to God's plan for my life?

Read **Chapter 10:1-21,** then answer the following questions:

1. What does it mean for Jesus to be Lord of my life? Do I experience any resistance? If so, where and how?

2. Faith comes from hearing. In this regard:

   a. How am I a good listener?

b. How do I share what I hear?

3. Who has preached or told me about Jesus? What effect has it had on my life?

Read **Chapter 11:1-36,** then answer the following questions:

(See "A Synopsis of Chapter 11" in Appendix II on p. 37.)

1. Am I secure in God's call to me, and how do I under stand and live out this call to be a Christian?

2. Who are the elect (remnant), and how do they become the elect?

3. How can God's remnant make a difference today? God never revokes his choice. How does this reality offer me hope?

4. How does God show mercy?

    a.   to Israel?

    b.   to the Gentiles?

    c.   to all humankind?

Read **Chapter 12:1-21,** then answer the following questions:

1. How do I understand my daily life as an act of spiritual worship, and how do I allow God to renew my mind?

2. How do I know God's will for my life; how do I use my gifts?

3. If I am to live in humility, what should my attitude be toward myself and others, and what would these considerations compel me to do?

Read **Chapter 13:1-14,** then answer the following questions:

(See "Justification" in Appendix III on p. 39.)

1. How does love fulfill the law?

2. In ordinary daily life how do I express the debt of love to God, self, and neighbor?

3. What does it mean to live in the light?

Read **Chapter 14:1-23,** then answer the following questions:

1. How do I respond to the cultural practices of others?

2. Since *"the life and death of each of us influences others"* (vs. 7), how do I see my life affecting others?

3. What is sin according to Romans 14?

Read **Chapter 15:1-33,** then answer the following questions:

1. *"The insults of those who insult you, fall on me"* (vs. 3). How can this truth help me to carry my daily cross?

2. How important is unity in the body? Is there a need for me to adjust my own feelings, thoughts, or plans for the sake of unity? How can I look to church authority, scripture, and a spiritual director for guidance in this area?

3. How did Paul live out his priestly duty, and how should I live out my priestly duty?

Read **Chapter 16:1-27,** then answer the following questions:

1. How have the support and prayer of others witnessed to me? Who were these witnesses and why do I appreciate them?

2. Paul warns us about false teachers. How can I recognize them and remain steadfast in the midst of them?

3. The mystery, kept secret for endless ages is now made clear and is to be broadcast everywhere. How do I relate to each of these parts of the mystery:

   a. God alone is wisdom.

b. The mystery, long hidden, and now revealed.

c. The Cross of Christ.

d. The call of pagans.

e. Salvation preached.

f. Restoration of all things in Christ as their one Head.

- Notes -

APPENDIX I

THE HOLY SPIRIT
AND SALVATION

Footnote "a" from chapter 5 of the Book of Romans in <u>The Jerusalem Bible</u>:
. . . "for the Christian who has received justification, the love God has for him and the Spirit bestowed on him is a pledge of Salvation."

Footnote "f":
"The promised Spirit distinctive of the new covenant as contrasted with the old, is not merely an exhibition of healing or charismatic power; it is also and especially an inward principle of new life, a principle that God gives (sends) (supplies) (pours out). Received into the Christian by faith and baptism, . . . this Spirit, the Spirit of

Christ, makes the Christian a son of God, establishes Christ in his heart . . . (It) is a principle of resurrection . . . which even in life signs him as with a seal, and which is present within him by way of pledge and of first fruits. It takes the place of the evil principle in man that is "the flesh," and becomes a principle of faith, supernatural knowledge, love, sanctification, moral conduct, apostolic courage, hope, and prayer. The Spirit must not be quenched, or grieved. It unites men with Christ and thus secures the unity of His Body."

APPENDIX II

A SYNOPSIS OF CHAPTER 11

The Lord reserves a remnant no matter how idolatrous His people become. Today, grace has reserved a remnant.

Vs. 8: *"The rest were not allowed to see the truth."*

Vss. 11-15: The Jews will be converted and bring about the resurrection from the dead. Meanwhile the pagan world is offered life.

Vss. 16-24: The root supports the whole. God will not spare us anymore than He spared the Jews. Holy fear of God is widom.

Vs. 29: *"God never takes back his gifts or revokes his choice."*

Vs. 34: *"Who could ever know the mind of the Lord? Who could ever be his counselor? Who could ever give him anything or lend him anything?"*

APPENDIX III

JUSTIFICATION

Justification is the event by which God, acting in Jesus Christ, makes us holy and just in the divine sight. The immediate effect of justification is sanctification and the ultimate effect is salvation. The foundation of Justification is the redemption.

Note: Justification is different from sanctification.

Sanctification is the state of holiness by reason of the presence of God within a person.

Salvation comes from the Latin word, "salus," meaning "health." It is the goal or end product of creation, the incarnation, the redemption, conversion, justification, and sanctification. To be saved is to be fully and permanently united with God and with one another in God.

Redemption is the act by which we are literally "bought back" into the grace of God by the work (sacrifice) of Jesus Christ.

- Notes -

- Notes -